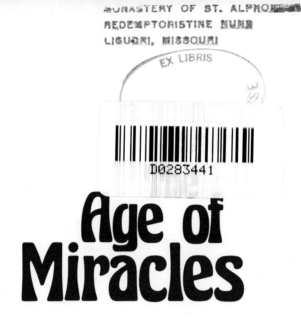

D0283441

Age of Miracles

The Age of Miracles

Seven journeys to faith

Morton Kelsey

Ave Maria Press · Notre Dame, Indiana 46556

International Standard Book Number: 0-87793-169-0
Library of Congress Catalog Card Number: 78-74095

Cover design: Joyce Stanley

Printed and bound in the United States of America.

To my friend, Andy Canale,
who has helped me and others
towards the miracle of transformation.

Contents

Preface:
The Victory of the Cross

At the center of Christianity stands the cross. By his resurrection, Jesus of Nazareth transformed the cross, an instrument of cruelty and torture, into a living symbol of victory and hope.

The cross of Christ speaks directly to the problem of human suffering. Jesus knew the worst of human agony and pain. Even those who are free of personal suffering look out over the continents of earth and see the cruelty and sickness, the poverty, and suffering humans everywhere. One question comes to me more often in my lecturing than any other: Why is there so much pain and suffering in a world created and sustained by a loving father?

There was a time when some Christians almost gloried in their suffering. Some even inflicted physical and mental pain on themselves so they could identify more with Christ's suffering. When we truly know the depth of our own being we usually find within us

9

enough darkness and pain to deal with. We need seek
no more. In 30 years of counseling, I have discovered
that nearly everyone carries a very heavy burden.
Human kindness helps us learn this suffering, but it
does not solve the problem of evil in our world.

Among the great religions of this world, only
Christianity speaks directly to the agony of the human
condition. The religions of the East usually suggest
that our physical lives are illusion. As we become
enlightened we rise beyond this illusory world and its
ugliness. In the West, secular thinkers from Freud to
Sartre tell us stoically to bear an absurd and meaningless existence.

There is no logical answer to this problem of evil
but Jesus Christ and Christianity give us a practical
solution. Evil and suffering are real. Jesus met them
and conquered them. He gives us a way to overcome
them with him. How victoriously the early Christians
heard and lived this solution. Persecution and death in
the arena did not defeat them. They knew the victory
of Jesus on the cross and they shared in it.

I have discovered that modern men and women
can be touched by the same victory and share in it.
How can we pass on this incredibly vital and encourag-
ing message? Theological language often leaves us
untouched. Stories, however, reach beyond our rational
minds and move the heart and emotions.

Jesus taught in stories and parables. In my book,
The Other Side of Silence, I show how story and
imagination can be used to bring us into a vital
relationship with the victorious Christ. In another
book, *The Hinge,* I have stepped back in imagination
to the crucifixion itself and looked at the power it

exerted on those who watched Jesus die on the cross.

One of the incomparable gifts of the Eucharist is that it allows us to celebrate the victory that Jesus won for us on the cross. In the Mass we participate in his suffering, death and victory. The church reenacts the drama of salvation in this central service of Christendom and drama is story in action.

Jesus told stories of the kingdom of heaven. He lived the same story in his life and death and resurrection. He instituted the Eucharist so we could continue to live in that story.

In the following pages I tell seven stories so that *The Story* may become more real to us. They are modern parables about suffering men and women who were touched by the cross of Christ and found victory. They are composite stories from actual victories which I saw take place in many years as a pastor. I saw many lives transformed as the cross came alive to seeking human beings.

I know of no other true comfort in affliction and suffering than the cross of Christ. He won the victory for us there and so gives victory over evil and suffering. Let us now listen to the accounts of seven men and women who found transformation in the cross of Christ.

Morton Kelsey
Gualala, California
All Saints' Day, 1978

Introduction:

Seven Words for Seven People

Calvary Church had been crowded with people from the beginning of the service. The church was stripped and bare for the occasion. The eight meditations were interspersed with times of quiet and prayer. Perhaps there were more people there on this particular Good Friday because a life-sized cross, built of secondhand lumber, stood on the busy boulevard to call people to stop a moment and think, to drop their busyness and be still.

The minister's meditations were not particularly inspired, but they were honest and sincere. He incorporated large sections of scripture as he told the story of the first Good Friday. He explained simply and directly the force of each of the words Jesus had uttered on the cross. He started with the Last Supper these men had shared together, in which they broke bread and blessed wine and pledged their faithfulness. Judas left when the Passover meal was finished and

it was night. Then, taking up torches and singing
hymns, the Master and his friends made their way
out of Jerusalem to the safety of the Garden of Gethsemane. The Master was in spiritual agony and he
asked several of his disciples to come apart with him
and watch with him while he prayed; the rest were
to watch farther down the hill. But they were all
tired, and the weight of the things which were to come
was too heavy, and so they slipped into the uncon-
sciousness of sleep while the Master sweated great
drops of blood. He came back and found them sleeping and asked them to watch again. How much he
needed some human fellowship that night, but they
went to sleep again.

Then he woke them and the soldiers were upon
them, and Judas came up and kissed the Master and
said, "Hail, Master!" and Jesus replied, "Friend, why
are you here?" Then the soldiers seized Jesus, for the
kiss had been the sign. A brief fracas ensued; a few
swords were brandished and the disciples fled into
the dark Judean night. Laughing and mocking, the
Temple guard pushed the man down the pathway
toward the Temple grounds where the Sanhedrin met.
There some of the elders of the people had been
gathered in expectation and a farce of a trial took
place. . . . False witnesses had been secured who
accused Jesus of Nazareth of the most awful blas-
phemies. The verdict was a foregone conclusion, and
when it was pronounced they blindfolded him and
buffeted him and told him to prophesy which of them
had hit him, and they laughed. All this time Peter
had waited outside in the courtyard only to deny his
Master three times. . . .

As the cock crowed they took him to Pilate, for
they could not carry out the death penalty themselves.
They accused the man of seeking to set up a new
kingdom, but Pilate was no fool. He saw through
them, and in order to release Jesus, he sent him to
Herod Antipas who had authority over Galileans, but
Herod only played with him before his courtesans
and sent him back to Pilate. Again Pilate tried to
free Jesus of Nazareth and he announced that, according to the custom, one of the prisoners might be freed
and which would the crowd have, and they cried,
"Barabbas." Pilate asked them what should be done
with Jesus who is called the Christ and the mob, egged
on by the priests, cried out all the more violently,
"Crucify him! Crucify him!" Then Pilate took water
and washed his hands and listened to his wife speak
of a bad dream she had had concerning this man, but,
giving in to the pressure of the Temple authorities,
he delivered him to be crucified. . . .

The soldiers took him to the praetorium where
they stripped him and flogged him. Then they made
sport of him and placed a purple cloak about him
and did mocking obeisance to him, saying, "Hail, King
of the Jews," and they plaited a crown of thorns for
him, forced it upon his head, struck him with a reed
and spat on him, and then they led him forth to
crucify him. His strength failed as he carried the
heavy crossbar up the hill of Golgotha, the place of
the skull, and a bystander, a black man, Simon of
Cyrene, was dragged from the watching crowd to carry
it for him.

Arriving at Golgotha, they offered him wine
mingled with gall to drink, but he refused it. They

stripped him, laid him upon the crossbar, drove the
nails through the fine strong palms, and then lifted
him to the upright which stood waiting and nailed
his feet to it. And so they crucified him between two
thieves. Their task done, the soldiers sat down at the
foot of the cross to gamble for his clothes.

The two thieves cursed and screamed, but Jesus
uttered no word until some hours later when he looked
around at the soldiers and the priests, the indifferent
jeering mob and the few faithful friends and said,
"Father, forgive them for they know not what they
do."

Half an hour passed and he spoke again, this
time in answer to a request. The thieves who were
crucified with him had made fun of him at first, revil-
ing and taunting him, but gradually one of them fell
silent. He saw something unearthly in this man dying
there beside him and he cried out, "Jesus, remember
me when you come into your kingly power," and
the Master turned his head toward him and gave him
the most sweeping kind of forgiveness that a man
could seek for, saying, "Truly I say to you, today you
will be with me in paradise."

Another half hour or so passed by and Jesus
looked down on his mother and beloved disciple
standing at the foot of the cross and said, "Mother,
behold your son," and turning to his friend, "Son,
behold your mother." In these brief words he told
them to go on, to cherish the common family bonds,
to continue them, to be faithful to them . . . all was
not over or lost.

Then came the most terrible cry that he or any
man ever uttered. As the sun disappeared behind

the clouds, so Jesus found himself bereft of man and God, alone, in agony, and he cried out, *"Eloi, Eloi, lama sabachthani.* . . . My God, my God, why have you forsaken me?" And then his body's agony welled forth as the traumatic thirst, the thirst of the wounded, forced from him the cry, "I thirst." A young priest came and filled a sponge with wine and lifted it to his lips and he drank.

Life was ebbing from him as he spoke the last two times. He uttered a strange statement often misunderstood: "It is finished." He spoke this to himself. His task was complete, brought to fulfillment, to perfection; it was finished. These were words of victory, not defeat. Then he spoke to the Father. With confidence and trust he spoke these final words: "Father, into your hands I commend my spirit." Then he uttered a great cry and gave up the ghost. The soldiers thrust a spear into his side and Joseph of Arimathea took down his body and buried it in a tomb nearby.

So the minister told the story. The meditations were over. The soloist sang. The plaintive words and the minor melody died away. . . "Were you there when they laid him in the tomb?" A heavy hush fell upon the church, a deep quiet. . . . The bell tolled; slowly one peal followed another. Thirty-three times the bell tolled. Then the silence of the politely attentive congregation broke as the people began to stir and move toward the door. Quietly the people slipped out and the church emptied. The minister was not at the door to greet the people. Without speaking even to their friends, the people quietly went to their cars and their homes. . . .

Most of the people had been touched by the service, though their lives would not be noticeably affected, but within the church there lingered a handful of people. They were hardly aware that the service was over. . . . They did not realize that the others were gone. They were deep within themselves. Something new had opened for them and they gazed intently upon the new vistas of an inner world, oblivious of the outer one. A hole had opened for them between these worlds.

The minister returned to turn out the lights. It had been a gray, gloomy day, dark and threatening. He saw them there, the seven of them. He knew none of them. They were all strangers. His first impulse was to turn off the lights and so invite them to leave, but something within him stopped him. He was tired. He was not the most religiously or spiritually developed person in the world, yet he could detect the reality of the Spirit of God when it was present, and the more he looked upon them the more awed he was. Something had happened in his church that day.

He sat down in the back of the church and watched. He could not help but smile at the seven people scattered there before him. They formed an incongruous group. There was a lady of middle age in a magnificent mink cape. Resting on her head was a hat of exquisite taste. Her bearing was one of easy elegance and power, the kind which comes from many years of directing others, and yet her face was streaked and her eyes were red. . . . Even now her frame was shaken with an occasional repressed sob, but strangely there was actually an air of release and joy about her. . . .

Sitting next to her was one of indeterminate age, as different as one could imagine. She wore no hat at all, and her hair had not seen a comb or brush in many days. Her unironed dress hung carelessly upon her. From where the minister sat, he saw nails that were black. She wore old and broken shoes on stockingless feet. There was an emptiness of expression about her face, and yet there was something else, a light of hope and expectancy quite different from her attire. In the last pew not far from the preacher sat a young man, not more than 22 or 23. He wore a sports shirt, khaki slacks, and engineer's boots. He was powerfully built and his face spoke of bitterness and anger. There were heavy lines about his mouth and eyes. He sat staring open-mouthed into space. Now and then his eyes would fall on the black-veiled cross, and he would bury his head in his hands.

The more the minister observed, the more moved he was. Such people as these seldom came to his church and seldom lingered long when they did come. He left his pew and walked quietly up toward the middle of the nave so that he could have a better look at the other four. These were not quite as strikingly different as those who hugged the back of the church. There was a man of early middle age in a rather garish plaid suit. His shoes were brightly shined and his clothes were immaculately pressed. An odd-colored tie, again rather extravagant, and a tinted shirt gave the impression of a man trying to be something that he was not. His hair was slicked back against his head, bright and lustrous. His face was rather blank, perhaps purposefully so. . . . He was deep in thought and noticed none of those around him.

Once or twice he knitted his brows, a smile came to his
face, and then he heaved a great sigh of relief. . . .

In front of him was a woman bent and deformed.
The wooden pew of the church caused her real dis-
comfort. She was dressed well, but plainly. The
pain which she had carried so long told on her face.
Her eyes were sunken and drab, her face sallow. Yet
suffusing this deformed creature was a radiant spirit,
almost a glow or aura. One could almost see the new
life pouring through her. Over by a pillar far from
the rest was a truly stunning young woman; her groom-
ing was fully equal to the beauty it heightened and
her clothes spoke of Saks Fifth Avenue or Neiman-
Marcus. She had natural poise. The minister had
noticed her when he had been preaching. One could
not fail to notice her. She had listened attentively
to his every word and was the very soul of politeness
to those for whom she had to move as the people came
and went during the service. Yet there had been an
agonizing lostness about her which her charm and
grace emphasized. There had been a dryness in her,
and now out of the desert of her soul a spring was
breaking forth.

One more remained, a priest of the church. His
black suit was threadbare and shabby. His vest was
spotted and stained, a crumpled gray felt hat lay beside
him. There were but few unknown clergy in the
vicinity of Calvary Church and the preacher had
spotted him early in the service. He had come in before the service began. How tired he looked and worn,
as if the burdens of the world were upon him. There
had been no change in him until the very end of the
service and then an amazing transformation had

taken place. It was at the end of the sixth meditation that his eyes had suddenly brightened. He had taken a deep breath and smiled, and then he began to weep silently, but they were tears of gratitude and thanksgiving.

For well over half an hour these people remained quietly in the church and then the minister had an idea. One by one he went up to the people who sat there and asked each of them to step across the street to the rectory and share a cup of coffee with him. Each one had accepted gratefully and soon the eight of them gathered in the rectory living room. A fire blazed on the hearth. At first the minister carried most of the conversation, but soon the charming young woman broke in, and then the lady of the mink cape. Quite naturally they all began to speak. They told seven amazing stories of how they happened to be in Calvary Church that Good Friday and what had happened to them. . . . Seven people had been transformed that afternoon as they paused to rethink and relive the events of Calvary so many years ago. . . . Perhaps there were eight, for the minister had never before realized the power of the faith he preached. Eight people made new friends that day, friendships which were to change their lives. . . . What were their stories? What had happened? These are the stories that they told that gloomy March afternoon.

I

"Father, forgive them for they know not
what they do."

Alice Maywell

It was the lady in the mink cape who had been first moved on that dark Good Friday at Calvary Church. Her name was Alice Maywell. She didn't know exactly why she had come to church that afternoon. She had been in church only a few times in her life. Going to church, as one of her friends had twitted, was "decent" in her set only for baptisms and weddings. As for God or Jesus, these words usually suggested that an oath was at hand. No, she was definitely not the religious type, and yet something had happened in church that afternoon . . . something so profound and wonderful that she could not believe that this was Alice Maywell speaking.

Her life had been occupied with every luxury that money could buy. Her father had started with one small grocery store and through hard work had made it into a large one. Soon it was the largest store in the small midwestern city in which they lived. Her

23

father then started another store in a city a few miles
away. He ended with a chain of 50 stores and a
fortune which made him a financial and political
power in several states. Her mother at first had been
deeply interested in the business, but something happened between them, and then they went their separate
ways, he in his business and she in her club work and
social activities. For their oldest child, a son, nothing
was too good and the whirl of parties staged at their
country estate was the talk of the entire state. Alice
had been born to them late in life. She was sickly at
birth and so she remained throughout her life. Her
father gave one look at the sickly infant and growled
that one could expect no better if one didn't take care
of one's self. Her mother gave her a little love, just
enough to keep her alive, and hired an Austrian maid
to care for the child. She wanted to do better, but she
had so much to do that she didn't have time. Of
course, the maids came and went. They gave no sense
of belonging, and Alice grew up the envy of the
countryside, and yet a most unhappy and lonely little
child. First she had her pony and then her horse
and then they sent her to the finest school in the East.
Two events stood out in her memory. Coming home
on the train, she met her father in the dining car and
her father was so deep in business or politics that
he did not even recognize her or, if he did, he did not
speak. The other was even more cruel. She had saved
from her allowance and purchased a really beautiful
picture for her mother for Christmas, only to find a
year later that her mother had given it away as a
present to a young chauffeur upon whom she doted.

When her father died, burned out at 50, he was

perfectly fair. Alice almost wished that he had not been. There was enough money in trust to give her an income of more than fifty thousand dollars a year. At 20 she was completely independent. She decided to live her life exactly as she pleased. She took an apartment, first in Chicago and then New York, and then began to travel wherever her heart desired. A few years later her mother died in an accident, and Alice found her income doubled.

She tried all the popular remedies for unhappiness, large cars, servants, beautiful homes, trips, even marriage. And each of these was as miserable a failure as the others. She found that most of her friends were looking to her for her favors rather than wishing to give real understanding. Even her husband had his eye on her money far more than on her loveliness and tried to swindle her out of part of her fortune. She caught him at it and they were divorced. Now she was alone. She trusted no one. She had no reason to.

And so she turned in desperation to the last popular remedy for unhappiness, the bottle. For the last ten years she had not been sober very often. Her money made it possible for her to get on. She was bitter and hateful. She blamed her family for what it had done to her, the world because it did not accept her, herself whom she could not tolerate. Indeed, at heart and core she could not abide herself, her own uselessness, for she looked upon herself unconsciously from the eyes of her selfish and indifferent parents. She could not forgive herself for making so little of her life.

Thus Alice Maywell fled from one place to

another. She had come to this area for the races. Her growing desperation and hate became more and more apparent to her. If she did not find some release, some happiness, she had made up her mind to end her life. And so, half drunk, she rode down the boulevard and noticed the life-sized cross and had the driver stop. "Is it nothing to you, all you that pass by?" "Is there any sorrow, like unto my sorrow?" These words on the bulletin board struck her. . . . She took a seat in the back of the church hardly knowing where she was or what to do. She knew so little of the Christian gospel that she hardly knew what happened this day or why so many people were gathered on a day other than Sunday.

The story unfolded before her. Her imagination was vivid and she could see him, the strong, virile young man, courageous and outspoken, the joy and admiration of those who knew him; she could see him deserted by followers afraid of the Temple, turned upon by the religious leaders of his own people, abandoned by his disciples, betrayed by one friend, denied by another, the laughingstock of the Sanhedrin and Herod, the pawn of Pilate, the sport of the soldiers and now hanging upon a cross. . . . She knew what he experienced. She had been upon a cross for 50 years, although she had taken much wine to forget it the last decade and a half. She knew what this poor fellow went through—but he not through any folly of his own, but because he was trying to live his life according to the deepest and best in him. This had only provoked the anger of those around him. She, on the other hand, had come where she was of her own choosing. She had had a dozen opportunities to change. Real friends had tried to change her, but those who disagreed with her were soon rejected. Stubbornly, persistently she had refused to look for any good in the world or see any in herself, had not allowed herself to love or care for others because she thought none cared for her. She knew what he felt, this pain of crucifixion, but he without blame. At least this one knew what she bore, even if no other knew. They would not now be worshiping him if he had simply died and that had been the end. This would be even too cruel for men!

Then came the first meditation and she heard the unforgettable words. Remember, she had never heard them before. "Father, forgive them for they know not what they do." He spoke these words to all who were there that day. . . . He spoke them to the High Priest and to Pilate, to the indifferent crowd who hadn't been present to cheer for him and those who had cried, "Crucify him," to the soldiers who sported with him and nailed him to the wood, to the jeering, sickening crowd that turns out for such things. She had seen a public execution in China. To all of them he spoke these words. Even to her he spoke them, to Alice Maywell, who had had many opportunities to discover hope and new life and who had gone her own way of self-hate and self-pity. . . .

There evidently was a Father to forgive, and here was one to offer the forgiveness. It came first as a little stirring breath of air within the closed tomb of her soul, this thought that she could be forgiven, and then it grew to a breeze and then to a rushing, mighty wind that swept through her. She could be forgiven, her parents could be forgiven for what had happened between them, for their indifference to her. As they were forgiven, then her own inner being, which they had not accepted, could be accepted by the one who forgave. So it dawned on her that she had worth and value, and she, too, could forgive the maids who had ignored or neglected her, the teachers in private schools who had punished her unjustly. She could forgive the friends who had betrayed her and the husband who had tried to defraud her, those who had grown sick of her self-pity and plied her with another stiff drink.

It was strange how quickly the alcoholic stupor passed from her, and how she saw things clearly, as they were. She was a child of God of infinite worth and value and meaning. She heard few of the other words that were spoken. She was remembering, feeling through the past, receiving forgiveness, and giving it. She thought of the many who had tried to be kind whom she had turned away, of the young man who had tried to show her that he cared and whom she had laughingly rejected, of the one servant who had really given of herself for her. No, her life wasn't as bad as it might have been and, what was best of all, it was not too late. She still lived, and with this fresh hard ground upon which she now stood she could make a new beginning. She did not have to end it all, but she could begin a new life and she would. She wept honestly for the first time in years and they were tears of joy and freedom. She had a chance.

It was then the minister came up to her and invited her to drop in for a cup of coffee. There she found others like herself. She could help this hardened young man to a new life, this broken woman who had sat beside her, who had not smelled too well, even the tortured priest.

I wish I could relate the whole of what happened after this, but that would be another story, of her settling down in that little city, of caring for others, of finding and ministering to old friends, of looking out for the miserable and hungry and cold. How many cups of cool water she was to give. "Inasmuch as you do it to one of these my brothers you do it unto me." It took years, but she became what she dreamed she might, a new being with a rich, full life. The day of miracles was not past. His wounds had healed her hurt . . . and her hurt, as it was being healed, healed others.

II

"Today you will be with me
in paradise."

Eric Adams

Eric Adams was no stranger to churches. He had been brought up in them from the time that he could walk. He had been a choirboy, had served at the altar, and been active in religious organizations, but for five years he had not seen the inside of a church except for his mother's funeral.

From the outside, people admired his family, but seldom do people see behind the masks we erect for the public view. His father was one of the officers of the local bank. They lived in the best neighborhood in town in a spotless, white colonial house. They were not rich, but they had everything they required. Certainly there was never any need in his home. Eric had a paper route and then an after-school job with one of the merchants on the main street. These were to give him a sense of responsibility. The family enjoyed many outings together. His younger brother and sister even now were still at home and happy.

The trouble started when Eric was about 15 and
started to get ideas of his own, ideas of what he
wanted to do and where he wanted to go. Up to this
time there had been real affection and understanding,
and then suddenly when he wanted to go his own
way, to live his life in a way different from his parents,
the great shock of his life came to him. His father
would have nothing to do with him. Either he would
do exactly what the father said or else he could be
on his own. To make matters even worse, his mother
upon whom he had always leaned would not intercede
for him. It came to him that she was really afraid
of his father. A conviction gradually formed in Eric's
mind that interest and affection are given only for
what the givers get out of them. He came to believe
that there is no such thing as love which has no
strings attached, no love that is not earned, but freely
given and freely received. How little did he realize
that his parents really feared that he might fall into
the problems which had plagued them as teenagers.
They were unconsciously trying to steer him clear
of them. The effect, however, was the same as if they
hadn't cared.

As soon as he could, Eric left home. Since jobs
were not very easy to get and since he could not face
returning home, he joined the army and was inducted.
It was at the time of the police action in Korea and
he soon found himself living under war conditions in
an impoverished country torn by war and famine.
He found himself with a type of person he had never
dreamed existed, for he had been much overprotected
and had very idealistic notions of what human beings
were like. War brings out the most heroic elements

in men, and also the basest. Eric saw only the latter.
He could not bring himself to join some of the others
in the evening sorties to the native village. He could
not be friends with those who did. He could not
bring himself to let others know how he regarded
such things, nor could he let them know how the
feelings welled up within him for the starving children.
He really thought that all real *men* were built of the
pattern which he had learned in high school, that
they were all he-men with no feelings or sentiments,
with no weaknesses in their impervious male armor.

It was then that the message came that his mother
was very sick, but he could not obtain a leave to go
home. He did not have the know-how or the in-
fluential friends. They did let him go when the message came that she was dead, but this was too late.
Then he felt terribly guilty about his leaving home. He
had not written home as he might have, as there
seemed nothing interesting to write about. He was
in a daze as he flew home and the daze continued
through the cold, formal funeral service. The minister
never came to call on the family. Eric went to see
him. He needed so desperately to talk to someone.
The minister listened to his story and said, "Buck up,
old man, with a fine church background like yours
and a fine family you will pull yourself together in no
time." This, of course, was just the advice he did not
need and it was what he could not do. He went on
home to find his father and his mother's brother in a
terrible argument over some property left by his
mother. He left the house, went to the Y, and then
went back to his base. He tried to erase from his
mind the happenings at home, in fact the home itself.

Back at the base he joined the boys and "tied one on." All of his pent-up animosities charged through him. He got into a mess and his partners in crime ratted on him to clear themselves. He was dishonorably discharged. His money gave out. He began to steal. It did not bother him. He reasoned thus with himself, "No one does anything for anyone else because he wants to, but merely to get something out of them. All life is a racket. All business is a racket. The only difference between most occupations and crime is that crime is more honest and forthright in its facing what life is like. Since everyone is out for the other fellow's skin, why not go out for it openly and honestly and take what you want." He developed this mature criminal philosophy after he was discharged. He found a cheap room in a large, impersonal city.

Since Eric was reasonably clever, he went on for some months without getting caught. He found some companions in this new venture, and then the law caught up with him and he received a stiff sentence in the state prison. There he learned more finished techniques of crime and perfected his negative philosophy. And yet he found moments of great unquiet in his heart, and he did not always sleep very well. He was determined, nonetheless.

He was released from prison on Maundy Thursday. He fully intended to seek out his former companions and apply his new education. He rented a bed in a flophouse in a small city not far from the prison. He put on a sport shirt and some khaki trousers and decided to case the town. As he walked down the boulevard, he passed the huge cross standing naked against the gray sky. He paused. Something old and forgotten was touched in him. Almost without his conscious mind knowing it, his feet were taking him into church. At the church door he turned to leave, but the thought of doing this embarrassed him, and so he went on in and plunked himself down in the back pew.

What was it that the music stirred up in him? The old melodies set something nearly lost ringing in him. How he had been moved by these services when he was a youth. He had served as an acolyte at them and sat through the entire services. Then his conscious attitude came back and he laughed, and the look of scorn came back upon his face. He looked at the people sitting there. "Hypocrites," he muttered to himself under his breath. He looked at the well-dressed man and thought, He is probably cheating his employees by poor wages. He looked at some young women there in a body from their office. Suckers, was what his look conveyed.

The minister began to speak. He had not heard the story for a long time: Jesus Christ "betrayed," the word came again and again. Betrayed by his family, for they had thought him mad when at first he started on his religious venture, by his friends, by his government, by his religion, betrayed, betrayed, betrayed. . . . He had never looked at Jesus in this light before. Here was one who had suffered exactly as he had, but how different was his response to his betrayal; instead of retribution and revenge, there had been patience, silence, forgiveness, endurance, and then resurrection. How he had loved the glory of Easter, the brightness and joy after the gloom and ugliness of Good Friday. He shook his head to push these thoughts out, but he had opened a Pandora's box of old memories and they would not be pushed down. He remembered sitting through one of these services with his mother, who always brought a pencil and a pad so that he might scribble when he was restless. He remembered her warm and loving hand upon his shoulder. There was a tear in his eye as they sang the next hymn, "There's a Wideness in God's Mercy." Again he made an effort to push away these memories. The conflict was like a cross within his heart. Then, too, he told himself, Christ had spoken forgiveness to all those who had participated in his murder, but Christ couldn't forgive *him*. . . . Look at his record of ingratitude, anger, revenge, bitterness, crime . . . everything from rape to grand larceny. There was no hope for him.

Then the minister began to talk about the thief on the cross, how in the midst of his agony he had come to himself. After railing at Jesus, he had really begun to see the man who was dying there with him and he had the courage to say (for it takes great courage to admit that one is wrong, particularly under those circumstances), "Jesus, remember me when you come into your kingly power." He heard the minister give the words of reply, "Today you will be with me in paradise."

It was at this moment that Eric Adams came to himself. The minister showed how much like the story of the prodigal son was this scene between Jesus and the penitent thief. Eric saw how his life had been that of the prodigal and here was the father speaking to him. If *this man* could be forgiven who had no chance to make amends for what he had done, how much more could he receive forgiveness and restoration. He made up his mind to go home and say to his father, "Father, I have sinned against heaven and earth and am no longer worthy to be called your son."

Throughout the service he thought of the things he could undo and old visions of life and vocation came back to him. It was not too late. No wonder he sat there silently in the church until the minister invited him to drop in at the rectory.

The woman who wore mink gave him enough money to go home. The minister put him in touch with a friend to whom he could talk in a city near where his family lived. Eric went home. His father and brother and sister received him with joy. He went back to college and then into clinical psychology. How easily he could establish rapport with men and women whom fate had broken. They kept him looking deep within himself. It took a long time before he washed out his bitterness and hate, but with good counseling and effort on his part he was reborn. The old darkness and fear would fall on him now and then, but at such times he would write to the minister at Calvary Church who would remind him of what happened that Good Friday.

Eric Adams rejoiced that the age of miracles was not past.

III

"Woman, behold your son.
Son, behold your mother."

Edith Rankin

In comparison with these other stories, the one of Edith Rankin was not spectacularly tragic, yet its consequences were just as destructive. There are many who may think that life is not as tragic as this cross section indicates. Sitting where I do and seeing into innumerable lives, however, I find that there is hardly a family which does not conceal some great misery, not a life which is well known that does not bear some literally unbearable agony. We fear that we are alone, and so we hide these burdens. Stop someday on a busy street corner and look at the faces of those who pass by and see how few of them are lightened with any real joy or purpose or peace. Most people carry a heavy burden. I will never forget the relief when this realization flooded in upon me. Yet only in times of crisis or real fellowship do the masks of men and women crack and slip so that we can see one another as we really are.

Edith Rankin had long lived in the city where Calvary Church stood. There was nothing unusual about her. Her childhood had been without any special incidents, and even the early years of her marriage had been uneventful. She came from the best kind of industrious working parents. Her father had been an energetic laborer and a fixit man in his spare time. She and her brothers and sisters lived in a simple but tidy home in a decent section of town. Her parents had even bought and paid for their own home. About the only remarkable thing about her parents was that, having a difference of view about religion, they decided that their children should select their own. That gave them the freedom to have none. Edith visited various churches as a child, but she admired her father, and his example of having nothing external to do with religion impressed her greatly. Unconsciously she decided to follow the father's example, as children so often do.

Edith was bright and did well in school. She even went to business school and had a good job before she fell violently in love with her popular, handsome husband. At 20 she was married. He was an excellent machinist and made good wages. Their family began soon, and she was far too busy to think of herself; a woman with four small children has to make time to have any private thoughts. As the children grew up, she was busy baking cookies for homeroom parties and served as secretary for the P.T.A. She noticed that some of her old drive was leaving her as the last child neared the end of high school. They had been good children and she loved them. She did not understand what was happening to

her, and so she closed her eyes to her feelings and
forced herself to continue the usual activities. Her
home had contained no more religion than that of her
parents. Oh, yes, they were very tolerant. The children could go to any church they wished, but if the
church asked for any money or suggested commitment,
they pulled the children out. They would not stand
for any such intolerance, but they were very gracious
about it.

The great change came after John, the youngest,
left for college. Edith Rankin was 53 then. She got
up one morning and she just did not have the energy
to do anything. She did not care. There was no
reason for feeling this way as far as she could see,
but nothing seemed to matter. She loved her husband
in a way, but he was busy in lodge work and spent
lots of evenings out with the men. They had grown
apart as she spent more and more time with the
children. He was no longer the dapper young man
whom she had married, but bald and with a pronounced "bay window." She lay in bed all that day.
Her husband came home that evening and asked what
was the matter. She said she did not feel well.

After a week or so her husband took her to the
family doctor who gave her all the tests and found
nothing wrong with her. She was in perfect health.
They even took her to a psychiatrist who spent several
hours with her and said that she was in complete
touch with reality and there was nothing he could do.
She would just have to snap out of it, but Edith
thought to herself, Why should I bother to snap out
of it? Why should I be anything else but what I am?
What is the use? When the doctor suggested shock

treatments, she had enough sense to refuse, for she said to her husband, "If there is nothing obviously wrong with me, why on earth use such drastic treatments?"

A year went by in agonized boredom. Now and then she got out of bed and went downtown. Her husband adjusted to the situation tolerantly. He ate out most evenings now and took one of the rooms which had belonged to the children. Edith talked over her situation with the friends she had, but all they could say was, "Snap out of it. What is the matter with you?" She lay in bed hours on end, read cheap novels or watched television. She no longer combed her hair or cared for her appearance. Her friends were disgusted and deserted her.

So it was on that Good Friday that she wandered, half out of curiosity, half out of despair, into the large church which stood on the corner not far from her house. She loved the chimes which rang from its tower. She was intrigued when they erected the huge cross on the boulevard. She had read a good bit and knew that it was Good Friday. Some religious knowledge is almost impossible to escape if you read everything that comes your way these days. Some of her friends said that the minister was a real nice fellow. One of her children had been rather active at Calvary Church. She was desperate in a quiet way. She was so sick of meaninglessness and its empty misery. She looked at herself and shuddered, but why care?

It was a strange story which unfolded for her, but it was not the story which affected her as much as the silences between the meditations. There was no television to turn on and no book to pick up. She

had to think. How seldom she had done this in the
last 30-odd years, how very seldom. She looked at the
other people in the large impressive church and
wondered why they were there. She wondered why
they cared, why they were not like her. Like so many
people she had gone on for years without ever turning in upon herself and asking who she was or what
her meaning might be. She avoided silence like the
plague.

The picture which touched Edith Rankin the
most was the one the minister drew of Jesus' last
words to his mother and his friend, "Woman, behold
your son" and "Son, behold your mother." Why
should he who was dying care about what happened
to them after he was gone? She was far from death,
and yet she found that she no longer cared for anything or anyone. Her children and husband got along
without her. What happened to them did not concern
her. Even more amazing to her was the response of
the woman, Jesus' mother, and the friend. They cared
enough for the dying one that they did as he suggested.
Instead of giving up everything because her son was
dead, instead of abandoning the cause because his
master was slain, they went on together. They acted as
though there were some meaning in life, as though
there were some real, tangible purpose, as if life had
a plan, a destiny.

The picture of the woman standing before the
cross on which her son died caught hold of Edith
Rankin. Here was one, she thought, with real reason
to lose heart and hope. She had been accused of forni-
cation or adultery, left with a son when her husband
died, seemingly deserted by that son who rose to great

renown and acclaim among her people, and now hung there on a cross, as a common criminal. Surely that woman had no reason to live, but she possessed some kind of inner certainty. During the silence Edith meditated on this. She, Edith, had no meaning, no purpose. This was her trouble. Having raised her family she had no function, no value, no meaning or purpose. She was slipping silently and slowly toward death and oblivion. Why should she care? If there were some truth to what this church stood for, to what this woman stood for, to what the son stood for, then there would be a reason to change. She had never before looked this far into her own life.

Out of the depth of her a light began to burn and a voice spoke, "Yes, I am here with you, if only you will turn and find me, but I am gracious and I force myself on no one." Within her being there was a purpose and meaning. It was her task to find it and let it live through her. She heard the rest of the story and the words, "Father, into your hands . . . ." She wrestled with something real and powerful, vital and luminous within herself. Something real was there. She wondered whether she could change. She wondered whether anyone would accept her or give her a chance to change. It was just at that moment the minister came up to her and invited her to stop by. It was all that was needed to start a chain reaction and nudge her will into action.

The rest of the tale is almost trite. It reads like some of the poor novels Edith Rankin read. She went home and ironed her dress. She went to the hair-dresser. She got out her hat. She came back to church

on Easter. It was like a new birth for her. She started
the confirmation classes which began the day after
Easter. She found the minister glad to talk to her and
give her books of an amazing kind to read, books
which made her soul grow and reach for new goals.
She began to help in the church office. She joined
a church group and helped put on a dinner at the fair.
The women accepted her and made no reference to
the past. Instead they praised her apple pie. She
began to share some of what she had found with her
children and her husband. He was so impressed
by what religion had done for her, that he even came
into the church himself. Edith Rankin began to live.
She became a person. Often the rector sent troubled
people to her and she would listen to them, give them
one of the vacant bedrooms for a day or so and a
meal prepared with love. Often this touched people
deeply and they changed, too. The age of miracles
was not over.

IV

"My God, my God, why have you
forsaken me?"

Norma Carter

Scarcely had Norma Carter begun to speak when she was recognized by the other seven in the rectory living room. This was none other than *the* Norma Carter, so often photographed in screen and video guides. Several of them spoke at once to ask her what on earth had brought her to the rectory that afternoon. She had everything a person could ask for. She had charm, success, a fine family, money, prestige.

How little we know the hearts of those around us; how little we suspect what they endure. She only laughed at those who asked her these questions, and she answered with several questions of her own: "What makes you think I am different from any of the rest of you? Do you think that having outer luxury fills the void of an empty life? Do you have any idea of the will it took me to film that last picture?" She went on to say, "I had come to the conclusion that life held nothing for me, that there was no hope until

47

I listened to that cry of anguish from the cross. I
thought that life should be easy, and in externals it
was, but there is usually an inner compensation for
outer ease. When the blackness of depression struck
me, I gave in to it. I did not realize that life takes
courage and that no one finds real life without struggle
and endurance. I was a coward because life required
nothing better of me.

"You all know my history. You probably know
it better than I do. My mother was the famous actress
and my father a producer. I was brought up on the
stage. I had all the right connections. I went from
success to success, from triumph to triumph. So many
people envy me my husband and well they might, for
he is all he is reported to be, kind, considerate,
generous. My marriage has been called a model and
no woman has three finer children than I have. Why
should I be miserable, so much so that only a month
ago I tried to take my life, only to find that I was
naive about the number of sleeping pills I needed?
My husband and the doctor kept it out of the papers.

"There were so few people I could talk to, for
one in my position has to be very careful not to gain
bad publicity. The depression first came on me about
three years ago. It came like a great cloud and
enveloped me, paralyzing my will. It was as if a great
ball of lead hung from my inner being. I had money,
so I canceled my next engagement and went to
the Islands for a rest. I soon recovered and began
to enjoy life again. Everyone was kind and helpful.
I came back to work, but soon the same blackness
came over me again. This blackness of spirit was like
the pain of an abscess, but the abscess seemed to be

on my soul. No one could give me the reason for it,
nor a remedy. I tried to talk to my husband, but it
only discouraged him and he would shrug his
shoulders. I went to talk to a minister who would
not even let me finish my tale, but tried to get me to
give a benefit for his church. I tried to talk to friends,
but they would not believe me.

"I had always attended church and thought myself a good Christian, but I thought of Christianity
as a golden rule of right living, of good counsel and
self-help directions. I thought of the gospel as sweetness and light. They never made much of the starker
side of the message at the popular church which I
attended. I did not think of the message of Christ as
a vital force to help one in extremity, but as a bit of
perfume to add luster to an already full life. I was in
agony that no one would take me seriously and had no
resources to help me. Even after I tried to take
my life, my husband thought it was an accident. Oh,
the letdown of writing notes and getting ready to die,
only to awaken perfectly well! No one would believe
me, and I was thinking seriously of driving the
Thunderbird off some cliff as I set out this morning.

"As I passed that cross standing unadorned on
the street, I was drawn to it. It was so grim. What
a horrible symbol for a happy faith, I thought. I saw
people streaming into church. I had never been in
Calvary Church, for I seldom came to this part of the
city. An unknown force directed the car to the curb
and stopped it. I can't say that I did. Mechanically
I got out of the car and locked it. I went into the
church. I was a little annoyed by the music. It wasn't
as good as in the big church that I attend downtown.

I was repelled by the story the minister told. It was cruel and barbaric, a story of betrayal, condemnation, injustice. The minister spared none of the gruesome details. I almost left, but something kept me there. The story he told, I had to acknowledge to myself, was the Gospel narrative, if you really looked at it. I expected the first three words. My minister had spoken a great deal about forgiveness and carrying one's family responsibility. I was not, however, prepared for the impact of the fourth word upon me. It shook me. *Eloi, Eloi, lama sabachthani . . .* my God, my God, why have you forsaken me? . . . It was strange the chord it struck. I had turned away from God because I had thought that he was interested only in sensible people and in helping those who helped themselves, and here I saw before me a new idea of God, one who cried out in utter desolation and agony, in dereliction and hopelessness. Here was one who could understand me, one who would not shrug his shoulders, one who cared enough to suffer what I was suffering, one who did understand.

"From the pulpit the minister had hung a crucifix, a small wooden one. As I stared at it, the lips seemed to speak to me and say, 'Yes, I know what you bear and if you will walk on, one step at a time, I will guide you through the valley of the shadow of death. I will show you what is wrong and I will bring you to new life, to a new creativity. Trust me and bear on through.' I must confess I was frightened by this experience. I didn't think that God still acted this way, that people had such experiences anymore in these rationalistic days. But this was the most amazing and solid experience of my life.

"Something happened at that moment. It is hard
to say what. There is no new meaning, nor do I yet
understand what my problems are, but from that
instant I *wanted* to find my way again, I realized that
there was a way if I had the courage to keep on it.
I sat in the church trying to figure how I could continue on the way which had opened to me, when the
clergyman came up to me and invited me to come
over for some tea. I am going to need a lot of help,
but at least now I know it's there and I want it. Isn't
that half the battle?"

Norma Carter was right. She was going to need
a lot of help, but she did receive it. She was wise
enough to realize that conversion is only the *first* step
in coming to life. So many people think that once they
are converted, they are simply to wait for "pie in the
sky when they die." The minister referred Miss Carter
to a physician of souls who helped her see how she
had gone against the very grain of her life, how she
had been interested only in herself and her success,
how she had forgotten others. The minister helped her
to see that God sometimes allows us to come to just
such a depression so that we may awaken and come
to ourselves and to him. He showed her that depression is not an entirely evil thing, for it can reveal the
abscess on our soul which needs treating. The pain
is trying to warn us so that our soul is not destroyed.

Norma Carter slipped back many times and
wondered many times if it was worth the trouble, but
she kept at it, sometimes railing at the newfound God.
But, strangely, the God she wrestled with and cursed
became more real than the one she had formerly
known. Gradually she came to love him and be up-

held by him, so much so that her agents were amazed at her new creativity when she returned to work. Norma Carter found the cure to her emptiness in a real God who demanded of her a different life than she had been leading, a real God who gave her compassion, understanding, rebirth. A God who reached her as he cried, *"Eloi, Eloi, lama sabachthani."* The age of miracles had not passed. The comfortable life of Norma Carter was not beyond the healing power of the wounded one.

V

"I thirst."

Edna Masters

It is strange that a cry of pain uttered by a man dying upon a cross could set in motion the healing of a woman who had been crippled by a sickness for nearly 12 years, but such is the story of Edna Masters. The minister had heard of her, for she was well-known in the little city where he lived and worked. She was one of those sick people not destroyed by her illness. She remained cheerful and active in spite of her pain and the increasing difficulty she had in getting about. She was admired by her many friends for her grit and determination. She was not defeated by what seemed to be the heavy hand of adversity.

She had every reason to be the fine character she was. Her parents had been active in establishing several of the social agencies in town. Her father had carried on a fine family business in a most exemplary

manner. Both her mother and father had been real
Christians, who knew their bible and practiced what
they read. When her mother died a few years before,
her father built a magnificent chapel in her memory
in their church. When he died suddenly, Edna was
not surprised to find that all of his affairs were in
perfect order. The business was disposed of and his
favorite charities were generously aided, while she
herself had all she needed to live comfortably. He had
planned his affairs so they would be no burden to his
ailing daughter.

The only real tragedy in her life had occurred
some 15 years before, and few people knew how
deeply she had been hurt. Even her parents never
realized just how much the foundations of her life had
been shaken. Edna was taught to look for her bless-
ings and to ignore her difficulties, and this she did.
She had been very much in love with a young man
who had worked for her father, so much in love that
she was sure that he was going to marry her, and had
let her affections carry her beyond her judgment.

The young man was equally in love with her,
but he was weak and not entirely faithful. Force of
circumstances gave another woman power over him,
and so without a word of explanation he dropped
Edna and married the other woman. If Edna had
any fault, it was that she was too good. Instead of
trying to find an explanation, she assumed the fault
was hers. She feared telling her father what had
happened, partly because of her own guilt, and partly
because she did not want to have her erstwhile lover
lose his job. Indeed in her heart she still loved him
and could not bear to have him hurt. Seeing that her

heart still went out to Don James and that she must
still meet him socially all the time, she drove her
feelings deeper and deeper into herself and pretended
not to feel at all. It was shortly after this that Edna's
health began to break. She had some unexplained
fevers and then came the crippling, progressive ail-
ment the doctors could not help in any way. Everyone
told her how brave and noble she was to stand up so
well under such burdens, and this encouraged her
to continue in an attitude of self-sacrificing nobility.

At the time Edna came into the minister's living
room she did not realize that this event of so many
years ago had played such an important part in her
life. She came to the significant realization there
that God did not necessarily will her illness and that
there might be a way out of it for her.

Two quite different factors brought Edna Masters
to Calvary Church on that particular Good Friday.
First of all, she didn't like the oratorical contests put
on by the local ministerial association in the name of
Good Friday. Then, too, she had heard that the new
minister at Calvary, although somewhat homiletically
crude, was sincere and that he held the novel belief
that Christian churches should be interested in faith
healing, an idea looked upon with scorn by her own
church.

She had been in Calvary Church for weddings
and funerals while the former rector was there and
thought it cold and impersonal. She was impressed,
however, with this service. The service increased in
meaning and power. She saw more and more clearly
the awful tragedy of that day, the terrible sin human
beings perpetrated on the Son of God. Some things

cannot be apprehended quickly; one must feel them
for a long time to appreciate their full horror. She had
never before sat for several hours as one man developed one by one the insults, betrayals, injustices,
agonies that Jesus had suffered that day. It came to
her more and more clearly that what Jesus had endured that day was wrong, utterly wrong, that this
was just the polar opposite of what God intended life
to be.

Then she heard the fifth word, as if for the first
time, "I thirst." These words summed up the physical
suffering of the Master. She had never understood
why these words had been the only cry of physical
pain from the cross, but now the preacher explained
that he suffered from traumatic thirst, the thirst of
the wounded, thirst caused by a loss of blood. He
went on to tell how men who have been wounded in
battle, as well as those torn apart in accidents, give
this cry as the very epitome of their suffering. She
remembered how her father on his deathbed, when he
had so many other things afflicting him, had spoken
only of his thirst.

It suddenly struck home to her that just as this
pain on the cross was a terrible thing and against
God's will, so was *all meaningless pain and suffering,*
that it wasn't just given to be endured, that it was not
God's will that she should have suffered and been
crippled as she had been for the last 12 years. This
man had died upon the cross to show the inhumanity
of fellow humans and to show that God could conquer
it. Could she imagine the risen Christ crying out like
this just to tell of his agony? There was more to it than
that. Jesus had tasted the depth of human suffering

and despair and the nadir of human physical suffering
in order to conquer it. It was almost as if she heard
these words ringing her heart and gathering other
words around them. "I thirsted that you might not
have to suffer, that suffering might be abolished
among the children of men."

As she sat there a host of ideas rushed through
her mind. Why had she suffered so? What could
she do? Where would she go? How would she start?
She had not even noticed that everyone else had left,
when the minister came up to her and said, "Won't
you stop in for a cup of coffee at the rectory?" She
had almost made up her mind that she would go and
see this minister, and just then he came to her.

She was quiet for a long time before the fire,
and then very tentatively and timidly she offered the
idea she had received from the service, and to her
surprise the minister said, "You are quite correct. God
desires the wholeness of every man, but sometimes
we get in the way and sometimes forces opposed to
his will gain control of us." She saw how others had
received power and transformation from the service
and she felt her pain diminish. She came back again
and again to talk with the minister. They soon discovered that she had long ago given up her desire to
live, that she had been living a false life out of touch
with her feelings, that she had hidden resentments
and guilts, that she had really hated herself and others
in spite of the mask of nobility and caring.

As she came to herself and sought to be what
she was made to be and wrestled with these things
conscientiously and honestly, not trying to be something that she ought to be, but rather trying to be

herself, Edna Masters became well. She did not leave her former congregation. She took the message of transformation back there in a way which none could ignore or deny. It was a long road, but she made it, for she discovered that the age of miracles was not over.

VI

"It is finished."

The Reverend
Alfred Darby

The Reverend Alfred Darby had been retired on a disability pension for nearly five years. He was only 50 years old but looked more like 65. His hair was white and there was a tremor to his hand. He spoke haltingly. He was a little more reserved in telling of his own life than the others had been. It is so difficult for clergy, because people refuse to recognize they too are human.

Alfred Darby had been looking for help for a long time, but he never found it until this Good Friday. He had been the rector of a very fashionable parish when he broke down the first time seven years before. No one could understand how such a thing could have happened to Al. He had the best recommendations when he came to St. Athanasius' Parish. He had been associate at one of the foremost churches in the East, and before that had been a curate in a fine New England church. He was a very hard worker.

He was very sharp intellectually, if not brilliant. No one could stand against him in a discussion. His sermons were to the point, incisive, thoughtful, if a trifle cold. The town went wild over him when he first came to his parish. No priest there had ever worked harder or more devotedly. The sick were continually called upon, the factions of the church were healed under his irenic disposition, and former members who left because an organist had been fired, were won back by his tact and understanding.

After his first year and a half in the parish, some of his more perceptive members noticed that he was more nervous and tense. Then the doctor ordered him to take a six-week rest. He came back full of life, but it quickly left him. He had to take drugs to preach, and then one day in an important meeting he blew up and said things which no one believed him capable of thinking, let alone saying. Again the doctor ordered a rest. Some friends tried to find out what the matter was and help, but it was no use. He made one more attempt to come back to the parish, and then resigned. He tried other jobs and simply could not handle them. The church retired him on a disability pension, but this wasn't enough for his family to live on, and so his wife and their five children went back to live with her parents, who had money. Alfred tried to live there, but he simply couldn't take their patronizing attitude (they had never approved of the marriage), and so he left his family and went to Chicago where he took a small room and existed from one day to another.

He tried to go to some lay people for help and their attitude was that, as a priest, he surely should be

able to find his own way. He went to some of his
clergymen friends in an attempt to get to the bottom
of his troubles, and the friends promptly went to the
bishop who called him into his office and berated
him for his weaknesses. There was nothing to live
for, but yet he lived on, hardly human.

A former parishioner had asked him to come
and spend the Easter vacation with him, and so he
came to the little city of our story. He always went to
the Good Friday service, although it embarrassed
him because they usually asked him who he was and
where he was staying, and he had to go through the
same sad story once again.

As he listened to the passion narrative unfold,
Alfred Darby was impressed more and more by the
courage of the Master. Instead of theological ideas
about the Christ, he looked squarely and directly at the
human Jesus. The minister had said one sentence
which struck home to him, "It is our task as Christians
to follow God's way for us as Jesus followed God's
way for him." This he, Alfred Darby, was not doing.
He had not had the courage to stand the turmoils and
disputes of his parish. He had not had the courage
to face anyone not liking him. He had been afraid to
go his own way. What he wanted to do was to have a
successful parish and to have everyone admire Alfred
Darby, the intellectual, hardworking, consecrated
priest. He never had the courage to find out what his
way truly was, the courage to go up to his own holy
city, to go through his own Gethsemane, to pass
through his own inner crucifixion. He had always
tried to protect himself and convince himself that he
was of some value, and the only way he knew to do

this was to try to get other people to like him. This
resulted in frantic efforts which wore him out and
made a physical wreck of him, which lost him his
family, his position and his self-respect.

Alfred Darby thought to himself that if Jesus
had been like him, everything would have gone well
until the Temple authorities began to cause trouble.
As rector he broke out in a sweat every time the
bishop's office called. Had he been in Jesus' place,
he would have gone into panic when the crowds began
to dwindle! Suddenly he saw his panic for what it
had been. It was cowardice. He was running away
as fast as he could by standing stock-still. His trouble
was acute fear, fear of facing the negatives of life.
Strange how much worse our fears usually are than
our actual problems. Difficulties cast long shadows.
He remembered how in those last days his heart had
begun to beat fast every time the phone rang. He
just had not had the courage to bear the tension, and
he had broken down.

It was his task to try to follow this man, Jesus,
and to try to have courage. It became clear when he
heard the words, "It is finished." Jesus had been able
to cry these words out upon the cross in the face of
every contradiction. He said, "I have completed my
task; I have done my work; I have done well and have
brought things to perfection." What were the external
circumstances? A rejected and deserted prophet
dying upon a cross between two criminals. He was
so sure of his own way that he could say: "It is
finished" (or completed), even under such circumstances. It was then that Alfred Darby received a new
impulse to complete his own life, to take it up where

he had left it off. Up until that very moment nothing
in that Good Friday service had touched him and
now new determination arose within him. He did not
know how or where, but he would finish his life, he
would complete it, he would bring his life to a satis-
factory end. There was a way. He would try again.

He sat long in church wondering how he would
begin, and then the rector had come up to him. Something new, something which had been dead for a long
time had stirred to life within him, but where he was
going he did not know. So Alfred Darby came to
the living room of Calvary rectory. That afternoon
he didn't say very much. The rector suggested that
he come back the next day. They talked and he
summoned up his courage and told of his inner fears
and turmoils and the rector listened, and smiled, and
said, "I know what you mean. I have been through
such things myself. Only I was fortunate. I found
someone to help me through." Thus encouraged, the priest told his whole story. How much
they discovered! He had been the pampered only son
of middle-class parents who had squandered everything on him. They had tried to make life easy for
him, and gotten him into places where neither of his
parents had ever been. Both of them worked so that
he could go through college and have the things that
only the children of wealthy families had. They did
the same when he went to the seminary.

In his teens Alfred had done many things that
would have killed his mother had she known of them,
for she was always talking about her wonderful son,
and about how considerate and thoughtful he was.
In order to forget some of his inner feelings and

attitudes (which he did not have the courage to bear),
he worked harder at school and received acclaim
that his impoverished soul needed in order to survive.
He never really thought himself of value, because
he was sure that his family would not have accepted
him had they known what he had really been and
done. Their acceptance seemed to be given only
when he lived up to their expectations. When he
married, it was to prove to himself that he could and
that he was accepted. No wonder the marriage broke
up as it did. . . . This story came out over the period of
many sessions with the rector.

The rector took him to the bishop, who understood, and then he began to help out in Calvary
Church. One by one he faced his fears, faced himself.
His courage grew. His way was not an easy one.
Many of the people of Calvary parish did not like
him. He continued to do what he saw was right nonetheless. Finally he invited his family back. This was
not easy, either, after four years of separation. He
began to follow his way as Christ had followed his
own. He found that going one step at a time, facing
each problem honestly as it came, taking the burden
of pain and humiliation, gradually restored his courage
within him. His vigor came back, his life, his power.
He began to preach sermons better than he had ever
preached before. It was a sad day for Calvary Parish
when the Rev. Alfred Darby was called to a large
and important church in that diocese. The work he
did there was the talk of the entire diocese. When he
retired many years later, only a few understood the
meaning of the words with which he ended his final
sermon: "It is finished."

These words had been before him through those years. He had a task to do that no one else could do and it was his job to finish his life. He, like everyone else, had a unique destiny. He must complete it, must bring it to fruition. . . . With Christ's example and help, he did. The age of miracles was not over.

VII

"Father, into your hands
I commend my spirit."

James Donally

James Donally smiled as he looked around the comfortable rectory living room. He had listened intently to what everyone else had said. He had not spoken at all. After the priest had told a bit of his story, there had been a long silence, the kind of silence that speaks of understanding and sharing and not of embarrassment. Then he broke the silence and said, "I see that I can trust you. Men and women who know one another on this level can usually trust one another. Do you know what I am, or rather what I have been?" There was a pause, and then he went on. "I have been for 15 years the tool of the Communist Party. In recent years I have organized your wildcat strikes and corrupted your public officials with money which I have received from the party. I organized the unemployed in the depression days and incited riots. I have fermented trouble and strife whenever and wherever the opportunity arose."

One would think that such a revelation would cause some comment among the group, but no one showed any amazement. So much had happened that afternoon that nothing seemed impossible. Mr. Donally went on: "I can actually feel a comradeship here in this room that I have been looking for all my life, but it is on a deeper plane than I believed humans capable of. I have seen today and I have felt today a depth of my own being and a response from others which I never knew existed.

"Naturally you wonder why I came to your service this afternoon. The reason is very simple. I came from pure curiosity. I had never been to such a service and I came to jeer and laugh. I knew the gospel story and knew that people worshiped this man on a cross, this pale Galilean. I couldn't believe that there could be such a glorification of weakness and I came to see for myself."

He paused and then went on: "Looking back upon the events of this day I suppose there were deeper reasons for my coming. I see now that there had long been brewing a secret inner revolt against the beliefs I held. I see that a soul as deep as this one within me cannot be contained forever within the limits of enforced beliefs. The communists fight a losing battle. You cannot war forever against such power and vitality as is hidden in the depth of the human soul.

"Do you want to know my story? I'll tell you. I was born 45 years ago in New York. My parents were emancipated people. They had broken with the church in which they were raised in the old country. They were laboring folk. Both mother and father worked. There was a large family of us living in two rooms on the lower East Side. My father was a brutal fellow. How my mother lived with him I don't know, but she was no angel, either. When the old man got drunk, he would beat us kids for the slightest boner we pulled.

"Then I found out one day that my mother was running around on the side. I hated my father and was disgusted with my mother. As soon as I was sure I could make my own way, I left home. I thought I had a sure job, for I was a good worker and the boss liked me, but the company went broke and I was out on the streets at 17.

"God, the things I had to put up with in order not to starve. I knew all the bread lines and rescue missions in the city. That's where I first heard the story of Christ. You had to listen to some of their sentimental hymns and a lot of sweetness and light about Jesus before they gave you a lousy bowl of soup. It made me sick, but when you are hungry you will even put up with creeps like that. The finishing touch was when one of the gospel gals propositioned me. I got out of the place and was complaining loudly down in the park when a fellow came up to me and said, 'We've been watching you and I think you could go for our way.' I was game for anything. They gave me a clean room and some good food and began to tell me their ideas of universal brotherhood and fellowship, of everyone sharing everything they had. Naturally I was sucked in. These fellows made a lot more sense than the people at the rescue mission, and no one else seemed to care. I had been good at school until I quit, and they started me out on my education again. They got me a job. Boy, I had to work that next five years. Ten hours during the day at work and then five to six hours in classes, and study every evening—for five years. I knew Karl Marx from cover to cover and Lenin and all their 'theology.' As soon as I was drilled to the satisfaction of the boss, I was given a bunch of fellows to teach. I was really sold. The trouble with you Christians is that you haven't studied your own ideas. You don't even know your bibles. You're lazy. You don't have any guts.

"My first doubts came when we all had to switch our line because Russia made a pact with Nazi Germany. It was easy during the war years when we were fighting together, but after the war it was harder and harder to go the party line. One had to bounce around like a rubber ball. I didn't dare look at my own ideas because I knew my whole life would collapse if I did. I did not have anything else to live by except what those guys gave me those long nights in the cell meetings. So when I couldn't stomach something, I pushed it down and worked all the harder.

"The first thing I knew I was rising to the top. If you work hard enough, you don't have time to think. I worked 16 to 18 hours a day. The real jolt came with the invasion of Hungary and I couldn't entirely forget this, but I worked even harder, and so they picked me to come to your little city here where the party had been able to do so little. It was a tough assignment, but an important one in the overall plan. I had some of the funniest things happen to me when I got here. I began to feel strange fears. I got scared to drive my own car. I couldn't sleep, even when

I was so tired I could hardly stand up. My stomach
began to give me more and more trouble, and the
doctor said that there was nothing that he could do
for it. . . .

"So it was that I walked into your church a little
before noon. I think that I was really looking for
something, but I would never have admitted it then.
I heard the story told with real dignity, no sentiment,
no eyewash, and it suddenly came over me that this
fellow, Jesus, had courage. He might have been
a fool, but he had courage. I've always admired
courage, always. This man walked right into trouble
and took the consequences without ever flinching,
without ever turning back. One thing they train you to
do in the party is to stick by your ideal no matter what
the consequences, no matter what they do to you.
This man didn't even have the party with him, in
fact he was against the party and he had the courage
to walk calmly into condemnation, abuse, mockery
and physical torture, without a word. He wouldn't
even take the cup of gall, and he didn't cry out on
the cross.

"You know, this Jesus of Nazareth captured my
imagination as I listened to these words he spoke.
How could anyone have the courage to forgive as
he did? And his words of forgiveness have lasted
while so many acts and words of hatred and revenge
have been swallowed up by history. I nearly wept as
he cried out, 'My God, My God, why have you
forsaken me?' He had such courage. It didn't seem
right to have the end come this way. Here was a
real man, no pale Galilean, a real man, strong, powerful, determined, with a purpose of his own. I heard

the cry, 'I thirst,' and the cry, 'It is finished,' but they didn't mean much to me. I was still thinking of the horror of it that such a man should have to die like this, pilloried on a cross as a public spectacle.

"And then he cried out, 'Father, into your hands I commend my spirit.' I began to realize that for him even dying on the cross wasn't a final disaster. At the end he had confidence and trust and hope, for he believed that beyond all this misery and inhumanity there was the Father into whose hands he could commend his soul. It was as if I were there personally at the execution and I saw him. I saw the look of peace and victory that came over his face . . . and then it struck home to me. . . . What was the purpose of my life and what I was doing? What did I believe? Would my belief help me in circumstances like his?

"I had been well trained and might have stood the pain in silence, but there would have been no confidence, no hope, no victory. I realized that even if we gained the whole world and had all people organized in communes, each man having all the necessities of life and time for recreation and art, we still had no meaning to give. Without freedom, and without some purpose to which they could commend their spirit, there would be no point to it all. I began to see how I was going to have to reorganize my whole life. I was a little afraid of what my former friends might do, and I wondered if the Christians would accept me. I was mulling things over when the rector came up and asked me to drop in at his house for a while."

The rest of James Donally's story is rather involved, and this is only a sketch. He broke with the party and went into hiding after two attempts were made on his life by his comrades. He went to the authorities and made a clean break with his past. Finally he was given a clean "bill of health." It took a long time and a lot of talking before he got to the bottom of his hostilities, hostilities which went back to his earliest childhood, but gradually be brought the whole of his life into harmony with his new insights. He began to read a lot. He talked with the bishop. He was not disillusioned with the failures in the church. He had seen far greater inconsistencies. He finally went into the ministry, for he said, "There is so much to be done. I know how men and women are hungry for meaning. Only one can help, one who knows the hopelessness of people and knows another dimension which can touch them. This man, Jesus, had what it takes. He became what we are in order that we might become what he is. The age of miracles has just begun."